Mark Van Doren
One Hundred Poems

By Mark Van Doren

MARK VAN DOREN
100 POEMS
Selected by the Author

AMERICAN CENTURY SERIES
HILL AND WANG • NEW YORK

To Dorothy

CONTENTS

vii

To His Book

Go straight to them, the sweet, the few,
That nourish, unaware they do,
The maker of these naked lines.
His solitude he reconsigns
To them, not him, as meriting more
Than he will of the final store.
For his most secret scowl and smile
He meant for strangers all the while.
Go tell them that, and call them friends
On whom his very pulse depends.
He does not know them save by grace
Of poetry's pure hiding place:
The charity in some to read
As it was written, and give heed.

MARK VAN DOREN
ONE HUNDRED POEMS

O World

O world, my friend, my foe,
My deep dark stranger, doubtless
Unthinkable to know;
My many and my one,
Created when I was and doomed to go
Back into the same sun;

O world, my thought's despair,
My heart's companion, made by love
So intimate, so fair,
Stay with me till I die—
O air,
O stillness, O great sky.

Morning Worship

I wake and hear it raining.
Were I dead, what would I give
Lazily to lie here,
Like this, and live?

Or better yet: birdsong,
Brightening and spreading—
How far would I come then
To be at the world's wedding?

Now that I lie, though,
Listening, living,
(Oh, but not forever,
Oh, end arriving)

How shall I praise them:
All the sweet beings
Eternally that outlive
Me and my dying?

Mountains, I mean; wind, water, air;
Grass, and huge trees; clouds, flowers,
And thunder, and night.

Turtles, I mean, and toads; hawks, herons, owls;
Graveyards, and towns, and trout; roads, gardens,
Red berries, and deer.

Lightning, I mean, and eagles; fences; snow;
Sunrise, and ferns; waterfalls, serpents,
Green islands, and sleep.

Horses, I mean; butterflies, whales;
Mosses, and stars; and gravelly
Rivers, and fruit.

Oceans, I mean; black valleys; corn;
Brambles, and cliffs; rock, dirt, dust, ice;
And warnings of flood.

2

How shall I name them?
And in what order?
Each would be first.
Omission is murder.

Maidens, I mean, and apples; needles; leaves;
Worms, and planets, and clover; whirlwinds; dew;
Bulls; geese—

Stop. Lie still.
You will never be done.
Leave them all there,
Old lover. Live on.

Why, Lord

Why, Lord, must something in us
   Yearly die?
And our most true remembrance of it
   Lie?
Until the pure forgetting
   By and by.

Why then must something other
   Come and grow?
Renewing us for nothing, save the
   Slow
Upbuilding of this bed
   Of needles, so.

Why is the soil not bitter
   Where we stand?
Whose, Lord, upon our roots
   The sweetening hand?
For so it is: we love
   No shallower land.

Dunce Songs

1

Where is the bell, the horn,
I hear as I go by,
Go by the invisible wall
That holds up half the sky,
The sky whose other half
Falls down like gold wheat chaff
And sprinkles all the air,
And powders my dull hair?
So people cry and cry:
Who wears that glittery crown,
That crown? And I say I.
Oh, what a falling down
As I go by, go by.

2

If rain rose,
And leaves fell upward—
Oh, me, oh, them
Sky-high together.

That is my house.
Here I am homesick.
Bright, oh, bright,
Forever, ever.

Raindrops, leaves
Round me like mica.
Snow whirls
In a ball of water.

Give it a shake.
That's me in the middle.
White, oh, white—
See now? I am laughing.

3

Some day,
When the great clock
Of dawn strikes, and keeps on striking—
What's gone wrong, the president will shout, why doesn't
　　　somebody,
Somebody stop it?—

That day,
When the music starts
That no man ever heard before—
Bong, bong, the bells up there, whish, whish,
The windy singing—

That time
Will be my time:
No minutes, years, no coming, going—
Night, poor night, laid out in white—oh, my soul,
The death of darkness—

Whee, whee,
The waking birds.
(Yet I do pity them a little—
Come close, I'm whispering—yes, I too will miss their brave
Songs at sunset.)

4

Then I'll be four-footed,
And modest with fur.
All over, all under,
Seemly and still.

Then I'll be patient:
A part of the ground.
I will go slowly,
And lowly—oh, sweet,

6

Then I'll be one of them
He that made all
Looks after the longest,
And tenderest loves.

Then I'll be quiet—
You can be quick—
And lie down all summer,
All winter, and sleep.

5

I have no enemy.
If I did,
I would wait for him, in the black dark, and thwack him—
Ha! on the head.

Or else I would grow
A green worm in my heart
And feed it all day till the strength of its poison
Was death to the world.

Yes, but I have none.
All are my lovers—
Harry, and Jack, and even the great ones,
That cause the long wars,

All are my little
Sweet friends that I wait for,
In the warm sun, and stroke them, stroke them—
Ha, my poor head!

6

Her hand in my hand,
Soft as the south wind,
Soft as a colt's nose,
Soft as forgetting;

7

Her cheek to my cheek,
Red as the cranberry,
Red as a mitten,
Red as remembering—

Here we go round like raindrops,
Raindrops,
Here we go round
So snug together,

Oh, but I wonder,
Oh, but I know,
Who comforts like raisins,
Who kisses like snow.

7

If I had a wife
I would love her as kings
Loved queens in the old days, or as princes
Maidens,
Met in the dew, by a stile, of a morning—
"How do you do, my pretty?"
And all of that.

If I had a wife
I would come home sometimes
Dressed like a stranger, and when she stared,
"Lady,"
I'd say, and woo her in wonder—
"How can there be such shining?"
And all of that.

If I had a wife
I would never be done
With remembering how it is now when, oh,
I am lonesome,
And no one is here but my dog and my cat—
"Well, old boys! Hungry?"
And all of that.

Pepper and salt
And summer savory—
Those are for luckier tables and tongues
Than my old woman
And I have.

The sun and the wind,
Those are our seasoning;
With maybe nine drops of rain on a Thursday—
Yes, my old woman's
A smart one.

She holds up her bonnet
Just when He is looking—
Oh, the love in His eyes, oh, the millions of tears.
Even my old woman
Is weeping.

Love me little, love me long,
Then we neither can be wrong:
You in giving, I in taking;
There is not a heart breaking
But remembers one touch,
Or maybe seven, of too much.

Love me more than halfway, though.
Let me think, then let me know.
And I promise you the same:
A little wild, a little tame;
Lest it ever seem long:
Tick, tock, ding, dong.

The Bird Desire

I took my gun,
I walked a mile,
And shot and killed
The bird desire.

Still it flew.
I shot again.
It fell to ground.
Desire was dead.

What then is this
That dips so near,
And on not two
But twenty wings?

No, a hundred.
Thousands now.
Where shall I hide?
Should I be proud?

I gave a mortal
Thing this life.
I made a god.
He multiplies.

He Loves Me

That God should love me is more wonderful
Than that I so imperfectly love him.
My reason is mortality, and dim
Senses; his—oh, insupportable—
Is that he sees me. Even when I pull
Dark thoughts about my head, each vein and limb
Delights him, though remembrance in him, grim
With my worst crimes, should prove me horrible.

And he has terrors that he can release.
But when he looks he loves me; which is why
I wonder; and my wonder must increase
Till more of it shall slay me. Yet I live,
I live; and he has never ceased to give
This glance at me that sweetens the whole sky.

The Translation

Ant and shrew
And marmot, going
Safely there,
The time of mowing

Comes tomorrow.
Meadow lark
And banded snake,
Then the dark

Sky will fall:
What is green
Above you now
No more be seen.

What is single
Will divide.
And as you run
The other side

Of all the world
Will drop its blue
As if it looked
For none but you.

Toad and cricket,
Worm and mouse,
You will find
Another house

That not a hand
Was there to build.
My own sky
Has never spilled,

Right and left,
And shown a new one.
Night and day
Mine is the true one.

Would it were not,
And could lie
Thus to the sickle
As I die.

Song

Spring of the world again,
Oh, is there such a time:
Eternity of April,
Past hills, past green?

There will be grass again,
There will be buds, be lambs;
Here. But what of the outer
Spaces fate lives in?

Good of the heart again:
Can there be such a spring?
You everlasting winter,
Does it come on?

I Have Come Home Again

I have come home again;
Not from so very far;
But love computes absence
As, star beyond star,
Worlds turn to nothing,
And chaos is there.

I have come home again;
Not since so very long;
But love measures meetings
As, song beyond song,
Joy turns to brooding,
And hushes its tongue.

Undersong

1

In wonderment I walk to music pouring
Out of so dark a source it makes no sound:
Not waterfalls, not wind, not eagles soaring
On wings that whistle insult to the ground;
Not insect whine at which the flower rejoices;
Not instruments, not voices;
Not, taciturn, those numbers where they wheel
While the fixed stars, creation's counterpoises,
Sing in deep throats a song of commonweal
More ancient than mankind, than beast or bird
Coeval with the Word:
No, none of these is what I overhear
In wonderment, in walking every day.
A harmony more hidden, as midway
Of the whole world it hums, and yet more near,
More secret in my ear,
Keeps coming to me, coming, and I know
As long as I go forth it shall be so.

2

Each day I walk in is made slyly one
By symmetries whose names I never seek.
For if I did, and found them, and were done
With listening, with looking, and could speak
Love's language with the subtlety they do,
It might no more be true.
For it is music's language, meant to please
No mind except its own, and if I too
Attempted it the melody would cease;
As birds do in the forest if a foot
Too suddenly is put
On pathways saved for silence, or for such
Plumed echoes as are proper to the place.
The music is not mine in any case;
I only let it come, by sight, by touch,

As often as by hearing; though the ghost
Of sound is innermost;
And mightiest, as if the great one there
Had burst his heart and scattered it in air.

3

Down it falls, that wild unfigured tune
Which nevertheless reorders all my earth.
I walk, and every acre is bestrewn
With witnesses of morning in slow birth,
And of the sky's contentment that things be
Just as they are to see.
Different were deadly, something sings
In a low voice as of a leafy tree
Preoccupied with shade, and two sure wings
That aim at it to enter by and by
When the half-day shall die,
And perfect sunlight shall hang due above
Like a dark lantern swinging. Something says,
Barely aloud, in less than sentences:
Just as they are, together in their love,
The whirlwind, the dove,
The contraries. Listen. That rough chord:
It is his breathing, it is our overlord.

4

In times of tempest when disorder seems
Order itself, the very rule of motion,
And moaning as they bend, the trees and streams,
In horror at their own perverse devotion
To chaos come alive, strain not to shatter
Form, and the first matter
Of which all possibility was made;
But then the roar increases, and winds batter
Winds above the world as fields are flayed
And savage grasses, blowing, strip the bones
Even of sunk stones;
In times of tumult when the lines should snap

That lead like silk from note to kissing note,
And the sweet song should strangle in the throat,
There it still is, miles above thunderclap,
As audible as when on halcyon days
It mastered the same ways;
Compounded of all tones, including these
Of stricken ground and hideous green seas.

5

And if there be those who would mock me, saying:
Music? None is here save in your head;
Noises, yes, delectable, dismaying,
But not in measure, as if more were said
Than owls and larks will tell you, or mad crows,
Or the wind-ravished rose,
Or human chatter, changeless year by year;
Then soberly I say to such as those:
The sound is one, and is not sinister.
It is an honest music through and through.
And so the chatter, too,
And so the silences that wait sometimes
Like a tired giant thinking, so they all
Return and go, then come again and fall,
Evenly, unevenly, as rhymes
Rival the pure chimes
Of never-ending truth, that for so long
Has sung to such as me this undersong.

Spring Thunder

Listen. The wind is still,
And far away in the night—
See! The uplands fill
With a running light.

Open the doors. It is warm;
And where the sky was clear—
Look! The head of a storm
That marches here!

Come under the trembling hedge—
Fast, although you fumble.
There! Did you hear the edge
Of winter crumble?

Posy God

Wherever a still apron,
Free of the stove awhile,
Descends among the rising
Sweet Williams, and a smile

Inhabits all the sunstrip
Betwixt woodshed and wall;
And then the rapid fingers;
And then the beetle's fall;

Wherever posy fringes
Keep time and darkness back:
Beyond the pump, the smokehouse,
Hotel or railroad track;

Wherever white and purple
Bring a brown hand to swing,
There is a hooded watcher,
Higher than hawk's wing,

Who folds his arms and listens,
Shady in morning shine,
To what he can remember
Of hum and bee whine

When flowery land was larger:
The center brilliant too;
All daisied, and all buzzing
Betwixt sun-up and dew.

7 P.M.

Slow twilight bird,
Suspended, as you sail, along the nearer edge
Of nightfall and the beechwood, are you heard
In places past my ears? Are you a wedge,

Slow tapered wing,
Driving into the outer walls of time?
Eternity is not so strange a thing,
At evening, when the towers that were to climb,

Slow searching beak,
Lie level with your progress in the soft
Dark-feathered dusk, and there are known to speak
Gentle, wild voices from the dark aloft.

Little My Soul

Little my soul,
How long will you live?
And where, if not here?
And why, if I die?

Little my life,
Who had you before?
And who will be next?
And again? What then?

Little my breath,
Did you never stop?
Were you never so cold
That known was unknown?

Little my soul,
You and I are the same;
Are warm, and are one.
Peace be till we cease.

High August

More things thrive in the sun
Than my sweet people and me:
The snake; the venomous vine;
The weasel; the wild bee;
And over us all sometimes,
Thunder, suddenly.

The world, put forth this while,
Threatens our breathing room;
Buzzes, and strikes; but then
Winter is soon to come;
We shall be few again,
And loving, and lonesome.

Midland

Under the great cold lakes, under the midmost
Parallel that Lisbon too lies under—
Vesuvius and Corinth, Ararat,
Peking and Chosen, yellow and blue seas
Enormous, then the redwoods, then high Denver—
Under the wet midnorth, under cool Canada,
Swings my own West, directionless; the temperate,
The tacit, the untold. There was I born,
There fed upon the dish of dreaming land
That feeds upon itself, forever sunk
From the far rim, from crust and outer taste,
Forever lost and pleased, as circling currents
Swim to themselves, renumbering Sargasso
Centuries a wind brings round the world.
There am I still, if no thought can escape
To edges from that soft and moving center,
That home, that floating grave of what would fly
Yet did not: my own boyhood, meditating
Unto no end, eternal where I was.

Only for Me

When I was twelve in that far land,
And was in love with summer nights,
And was in love with Linda Jane,
Whose very name was dancing lights
About my dark, my country bed,
Once I dreamed that she was dead.

And woke; and not one window star,
As I looked out, but wept for me.
I looked again, and my own tears,
Like magic lanterns, made me see
The very eyes of Linda Jane
Weeping everywhere like rain.

Then the sunrise, cool and red,
And then the new day, white and hot.
And after that the growing up
And the forgetting—oh, but not
The selfless woe of one that died.
Only for me, for me she cried.

No Word, No Wind

I

What god was there
When the slow buggy, appearing and disappearing,
Slipped in and out of moon and maple shadows, down
Those least of earth's depressions, up those low,
Those prairie rises? Eighteen miles
From town to sleepy town, and not a lamp
In any passing window—oh, so slowly
Passing, as the mare's feet
Shuffled, and the delicate wheels
Answered, invisible in windless
Dust. No weather then,
No breath of any god, no loud intelligence
Looking. Nothing blown out of the north,
No word.
What understanding, nevertheless, what hidden listener
Brooded? For the whole of that great place
Consented—I remember it—
Consented, and we nodded in the narrow
Seat, and safely crawled up hills
That were no hills, down grades that were but folded
Ground, with gentle pockets of cool air
Where the night sighed, considering itself.
No rain, no sun, no sting of snow,
No sound of rivers, sluggish, far away among their sycamores
In bottom land, forgotten.
And no wind.
What god, if nothing breathed? I might go back there,
Maybe, and find out. But that same night
Is not there now;
Never again, I think, will such a stillness
Be, and not be spoken to.
No word, no wind—I swear it,
Not one sign
That the world knew we went that way at all.

Whereas in whirling March—oh, I remember—
Or the dog days,
Or knee deep in the Christmas drifts
That crusted later—all white ice
Both ways a thousand miles to where the mountains were,
And are, that leave that valley to itself,
Lonesome, and vast, and unreportable—
Or mournfully, in fall,
When the pale corn, suffering the southwest
Trade winds, rustled by night, by day, as if à dead sea
Whispered, pitying the labor
Of its own waves, interminable, intentless—
Then what mind presided? Father
Or mother of all those men,
Those midland children, what lost mind
Like theirs looked down and listened,
Sharing it with them, that great place
To which they both consented? Someone did,
And does. Or are they several, enormous, many-
Minded, with no single
Voice that yet can sing, that yet can say,
As some day it may do, what meaning lies
In the long vacancy between those silent mountains?
So far, not a thoughtful
People; so far, not an articulate
Deity, unless that world of weather
Itself is god, is goddess, trying
Their patience whom alternately it blasts
And lulls to slumber
On hot nights
When grain but not idea grows. I might go back there,
Maybe, and look sharp; and shall,
Some day, and listen. There is no other
Sky that I would rather, after these distant
Years, see face to face.

Homer, Sidney, Philo

Homer, Sidney, Philo,
Strung along the Wabash:
Beads in the black land.
Corn grows, but no change
In these little towns.

After forty springtimes
Nothing to look out at.
Seven miles, eight miles—
Strangers in the blue express
Yawn and despise them.

So would I, certainly,
Except that I remember
Homer Park on hot days.
We took the interurban.
We kissed in the shade.

Sidney was our junction;
Six trains a week there.
We rode the dusty local—
Opening all windows—
Then to Detroit.

Philo we drove through,
Cold nights, with horses.
Once there was a dim lamp
Showing, and my father
Stopped for oyster stew.

After forty autumns,
Only I am different.
Here they are as always;
They cannot remember
Themselves as I do.

Family Prime

Our golden age was then, when lamp and rug
Were one and warm, were globe against the indifferent
Million of cold things a world contains.
None there. A light shone inward, shutting out
All that was not corn yellow and love young.

Like winter bears we moved, our minds, our bodies
Jointed to fit the roundness of a room:
As sluggish, and as graceful, whether couch
Or table intercepted, or if marbles
Clicked on the floor and hunched us into play.

How long? I do not know. Before, a blank.
And after, all this oldness, them and me,
With the wind slicing in from everywhere,
And figures growing small. I may remember
Only a month of this. Or a God's hour.

Yet I remember, and my father said
He did: the moment spherical, that age
Fixes and gilds; eternity one evening
Perfect, such as maybe my own sons,
And yours, will know the taste of in their time.

The Cornetist

When the last freight, dusk-musical, had gone,
Groaning along the dark rails to St. Louis,
When the warm night, complete across the cornfields,
Said there was nothing now, no motion left,
No possible sound, we heard him:
Rocked on the silent porch and heard the low notes

Leave on their level errand like the last sound
Ever to be man-blown about the earth.
Like the last man this sentry of the switches
Blew, and the mournful notes, transcending cinders,
Floated above the corn leaves:
Floated above the silks, until arriving,

Arriving, they invaded our warm darkness,
Deep in the still verandah, and we laughed:
"Why, there he is, that pitiful lone devil;
There is the Frisco nightingale again,
There is our mocking-bird-man"—
Laughed, and said these things, and went to bed.

And slept; but there are nights now when I waken,
After these years, and all these miles away,
When I sit up and listen for the last sound
Man will have made alive; and doubt a little
Whether we should have laughed;
Whether we should have pitied that poor soul.

You were too sure of being there forever,
And I too soon was leaving to be wise.
Not that his horn had wisdom; but at nighttime
Man has a need of man, and he was there,
Always; the horn was there
Always; and joy, I think, was why we laughed.

And slept; for there is many an hour of drearness,
Many an hour unloud with lips or brass,
When I lie still and listen for the last note
Ever some lung has blown; and am self-envious,
Thinking I once could laugh;
Thinking I once could pity that poor soul.

Civil War

The country is no country I have seen,
And no man goes there who is now alive, and no man
Ever is going to leave there. But they try;
Waving a million beards that on pale faces
Blacken with time and spread.
It is a field of bodies of blue boys,
And grey boys, grown half way into the ground.
The wind is dark that sways them;
All of them bending with it, south or north,
All of them straining here; but no one knowing
Of any fellow by who gazes too.
It is a field of legless bearded boys
With bright unnecessary buttons on their breasts,
And skirts of coats that hold them in the sod.
The bodies twist,
The circular, small eyes are mad with being;
A million mouths fly open without sound;
But none can tear his coat up, that must come
With roots and worms or come not up at all.

Away in Carolina, Maine, Wisconsin,
Boys who kept their legs walked long and long.
They set their feet in furrows, or in aisles;
They strolled with girls, were taken, and were fathers;
Had old companionship; and last were covered
Quietly with smooth boards, and grass, and stone.
Stiffly now they hold society;
Forever thus they lie without a want.

In the forbidden country where the sod
Grows down and down, with restless blue roots, grey roots,
In the dark windy land no one can leave,
Separate necks yearn homeward;
Separate hungry shoulders pull and pull.
Wind, oh wind, I did not come to stay;
I must be there tomorrow, not to miss—
But the dark wind is earless, and the day
Is endless, and the grasses hiss and hiss.

This Amber Sunstream

This amber sunstream, with an hour to live,
Flows carelessly, and does not save itself;
Nor recognizes any entered room—
This room; nor hears the clock upon a shelf,
Declaring the lone hour; for where it goes
All space in a great silence ever flows.

No living man may know it till this hour,
When the clear sunstream, thickening to amber,
Moves like a sea, and the sunk hulls of houses
Let it come slowly through, as divers clamber,
Feeling for gold. So now into this room
Peer the large eyes, unopen to their doom.

Another hour and nothing will be here.
Even upon themselves the eyes will close.
Nor will this bulk, withdrawing, die outdoors
In night, that from another silence flows.
No living man in any western room
But sits at amber sunset round a tomb.

The Animals

So cunningly they walk the world,
So decently they lay them down,
Who but their maker sees how pride
And modesty in them are one?

These that did not conceive themselves,
Nor dream how long ago it was,
Have yet no deeper joy by night,
By day, than to continue thus.

The patience in them, and the heat,
The languor, then the sudden life:
Body and soul identical,
Their secret is forever safe.

Oh mystery, Oh perfect grace:
Duty as instant as desire;
Nature and art so indistinct
A wonder even in heaven were.

Spring Birth

The lord of increase, traveling with me,
Said: "Look! There are more than you will see,
Yet look!" And laughed, and pointed at the small
Pigs bouncing as they ran, and at the tall
Bewildered foals, their four legs wildly braced
Lest the ground heave again; while kittens chased
White butterflies, and calves, all ears and head,
Butted and sucked as their great mothers fed.
The lord of increase grinned. "A few of mine,
With foster-help. But listen!" And the whine
Of mayflies filled my ears, and far away,
In wilderness, eggs opened unto day,
And little serpents—were they noiseless?—slid
Through the warm sand. Bare birds above them hid,
Faint-peeping, and a hornet lifted wing
For the first time in nature—not to sting,
But trying the blue air. "All these, and more.
Now close your eyelids." And the forest floor
Padded with feet of foxes, old and young,
As ugly owlets blinked, and beetles clung
To ridges of last winter's bark. "More yet?"
But I believed him, lord of all beget.

Animal-Worship

Once on this ancient plain there fell the shade
Of a great loping hare who hid the sun;
Who darkened the high sky; and has not made
Another unearthly visit since that one.

Even that day is dead; no solemn eyes
Remain of those that watched him down the North;
Or those that feasted yearly, Indian wise,
On the small furless copies he sent forth:

The timorous rabbits, ancient on this plain,
Who now no more bring messages of cold;
Sons of the great mild hare whose dozing brain
At the world's upper edge grows dimly old.

In a sunk nest of snow he lies and dreams;
Down a grey depth he slumbers, long from here;
While the plowed plain forgets him, and the teams
Trample, and fatherless rabbits shake with fear.

No longer does their blood remember time,
No longer do they feel their far descent;
As the loud valley crows cry out and climb,
Sky-highward, where the one great raven went,

So long ago, so darkly through these hills,
That the last man is buried who was told;
That the last wing is mildewed, and the bills
Of once deep-knowing birds are green with mould.

So the loud western crow wings flap and lift,
And sagely now the beaks consider corn;
But none of them remembers here the swift
Vast body whence their images were born.

Past a blue mountain, westernmost of all,
He floats among the mist-pools, round and round;
And meeting the Hawk, floats on; no feathers fall;
For they go by, those gods, without a sound.

There is no beast or bird too delicate now
For man's vain understanding; no shod feet
Veer shyly from their pathways; no heads bow
Benignly when a man and serpent meet.

No creature upon four paws, in field or wood,
By rivers or by runways, stares and wins:
His muteness meaning wisdom, and his hood
Some heraldry of old where birth begins,

Where truth, where secret might, where sun and moon,
Where song and words of song, and what to pray.
There was a time when foxes set the tune;
And tigers; but it is another day.

It is the beasts' oblivion, when they run
Uncounted unto cover; when they shrink,
Denying their tall origin; when one
Trots lonely in the dew that he will drink;

When two by two they wander, with no word
Between them of the Hawk, the burrowed Hare;
The Raven, or the Bullock, or the herd
Of tempest-laughing Stallions, or the Bear.

One only of earth's animals is proud;
One only of its movers can be still.
Man only sits at rest and sees the crowd
File curving by, deflective to his will;

Sits on and sees, with nothing spread above,
No weird ancestral wing, no hovering mane;
Sits loftily, too certain of self-love
Ever to see a world upon the wane:

His world and theirs, the strangers whom he knows
Forgetfully, from their own selves disguised.
Man is time's fool, who withers the wild rose
Of that young day when gods were recognized.

The Distant Runners

*Six great horses of Spain, set free after
his death by De Soto's men, ran West
and restored to America the wild race
lost there some thousands of years ago.*
—LEGEND.

Ferdinand De Soto lies
Soft again in river mud.
Birds again, as on the day
Of his descending, rise and go
Straightly West, and do not know
Of feet beneath that faintly thud.

If I were there in other time,
Between the proper sky and stream;
If I were there and saw the six
Abandoned manes, and ran along,
I could sing the fetlock song
That now is chilled within a dream.

Ferdinand De Soto, sleeping
In the river, never heard
Four-and-twenty Spanish hooves
Fling off their iron and cut the green,
Leaving circles new and clean
While overhead the wing-tips whirred.

Neither I nor any walker
By the Mississippi now
Can see the dozen nostrils open
Half in pain for death of men;
But half in gladness, neighing then
As loud as loping would allow.

On they rippled, tail and back,
A prairie day, and swallows knew
A dark, uneven current there.
But not a sound came up the wind,
And toward the night their shadow thinned
Before the black that flooded through.

If I were there to bend and look,
The sky would know them as they sped
And turn to see. But I am here,
And they are far, and time is old.
Within my dream the grass is cold;
The legs are locked; the sky is dead.

A Deer Is Feeding

A deer is feeding in the orchard grass:
A doe; with young ears, maybe, watching her
From the pine thicket southward; not to stir
Until she starts; and then the two will pass,
On amber ankles, delicate as glass,
Among great stones and trees, by dust and burr
Unbothered; or by me—oh, foreigner
Forever, and most terrible, alas.

See how she looks and fears me, all her skin
Atremble. But her eyes—I know them best,
From some that I saw dying once. Within,
How dark, without, how moist. What agony,
What dew of old despair, that even we
Who love them cannot ever burn to rest.

December Cats

Less and less they walk the wild
Cold world of dark, of windy snow.
Curiosity comes in;
There is nothing more to know;
Examines corners; yawns and dies,
Warm under lamps and buzzing flies.

The oldest beast, with panther head,
The latest yielded: ran in tracks
Himself had punctured; hid by stones,
And pounced, and crackled mice's backs.
But now that all midwinter wests,
Even he the ranger rests.

And Did the Animals?

And did the animals in Noah's ark—
That was of oleander wood, with cabins
Cunningly bitumined in and out—
Did all those animals lie quietly?
For months and weeks and days, until the dove
Came home, and they were dry on Ararat,
Did every bird, with head beneath its wing,
Did every beast, with forepaws folded in,
Did every reptile, coiled upon itself,
Lie sleeping as no man did, patiently?
A man might think this tempest would not end,
Nor timbers cease to creak, nor the light come.
These did not know it rained, these did not know
Their kind survived in them if it survived.
A thinking man might doubt it, and in misery
Listen. Did they listen? But to what?
They did not know of time, they did not count
The waves. Then did they cry out in their dreams?
Or did they even dream, those specimen souls?

Former Barn Lot

Once there was a fence here,
   And the grass came and tried,
Leaning from the pasture,
   To get inside.

But colt feet trampled it,
   Turning it brown;
Until the farmer moved
   And the fence fell down.

Then any bird saw,
   Under the wire,
Grass nibbling inward
   Like green fire.

Under This Building

Under this building
A small stream runs,
In the dark, and noiseless
Save for a frog—
Listen, that lets me
Know he is there.
Not now; he is waiting;
He takes his time.

I must not wait;
He will never begin.
It is not for me
His intervals are,
It is not to me
He says what he says,
Or to anyone warm—
Ah, there he is.

After Dry Weather

If the people under that portico
Are happy, and point at the pattering drops;
If barehead boys are parading below
Musical eaves of tall house-tops;

If you lean out of the window here,
Contented so with the pavement's shine,
And laugh as the covers of cabs appear
With passengers in them dressed to dine;

If all of the stones that we can see
Are licking their lips, that waited so long,
A meadow I know to the north of me
By a hundred miles has caught the song.

I am certain the clover has lifted its head
For dark, intemperate draughts of rain.
Once even I thought I had heard the tread
Of a plunging horse with a sodden mane.

After Long Drought

After long drought, commotion in the sky;
After dead silence, thunder. Then it comes,
The rain. It slashes leaves, and doubly drums
On tin and shingle; beats and bends awry
The flower heads; puddles dust, and with a sigh
Like love sinks into grasses, where it hums
As bees did once, among chrysanthemums
And asters when the summer thought to die.

The whole world dreamed of this, and has it now.
Nor was the waking easy. The dull root
Is jealous of its death; the sleepy brow
Smiles in its slumber; and a heart can fear
The very flood it longed for, roaring near.
The spirit best remembers being mute.

Orion: October

As firelogs hiss, Orion gleams
Recumbent in the eastern cold;
And did when not a roof was here,
Nor any brain to think him old.

We go outdoors in fall and stare
At each of his great seven stars,
And number all the sunken ships
It witnessed, all the risen wars.

But he was there when not an eye
Looked into his, when not an earth.
No direction yet was named
When that deep universe had birth.

Nor cold nor hot. How white he is,
How ancienter than frost or fire.
We go back in. We shut him out.
Oblivion's sons forget the sire.

Now the Sky

How long have standing men, by such a stone
As this I watch from on this windless night,
Beheld Arcturus, golden and alone,
Guiding Antares and the Snake aright.

The Scales were up when not an Arab walked
On sand that soon was paved with names of stars;
Boötes herded, and the Giant stalked
Past the curved Dragon, contemplating wars.

How many an open eye, bedight with dew,
Over the sleeping flowers has drawn them down:
Andromeda, and Berenice's few
Dim tresses that shall ever flee the Crown.

From such a rock whence greybeards long ago,
Forgetting it beneath them, heard the Lyre,
I watch. But there is something now we know
Confusing all they saw with misty fire.

For them a hundred pictures on a slate.
For us no slate, and not a hand that draws.
For them a pasture-dome wherefrom the gate
Of Cancer led the Lion through its claws.

For them a frosty window, painted over,
Nightly, with flower faces in a ring:
Daisies dancing up, and clouds of clover
Scenting the after way, and phlox to fling

Thin petals left and right till morning lifted.
For us no shapely flame in all the dark;
For us a million embers that have drifted
Since the first fire, and not a sign to mark

Where anything shall end, or which shall go
With which until they both shall die to grey.
For watchers once a changeless face to know;
For us cold eyes that turn henceforth away.

They saw each constellation take its hour
Of triumph overhead, before it started
Down the broad West, whereon the death of power
Was written by the Ram, and nightly charted.

The Eagle and the Swan, that sailed so long,
Floating upon white wings the Arrow missed,
Tilted at midnight, plunging with a song
Earthward, and—as they sank—deep Hydra hissed.

Leo had long been growling in his lair
When Pegasus neighed softly in the East,
Rising upon a wind that blew his hair
Freshly, until Aquarius increased

The stream he aimed against the Fish's mouth,
And all the stars were wet with silent rain.
The Hyades came weeping, and the South
Sent mist to soothe the Sisters in their pain.

These things they witnessed, and Orion, climbing
Fiercely with those two Dogs announcing Fall;
Then Winter, with Aldebaran loud-chiming,
Baiting the frozen Bull, that turned to call

The Bears to warm his anger. These they knew,
And knew the seasons with them, Spring and Spring;
Counting the dozen signs the finger drew
That swung the inconstant Sun around the Ring.

Slow Jupiter proceeded as they planned,
Lingering among the Twelve in stately turn;
They touched the breasts of Venus, where the hand
Of Mars's fiery love had been to burn.

The sky was then a room, with people going
Faithfully to and fro, and beasts enchained.
The sky was then a midnight wastrel, throwing
Riches away; and still the purse remained.

But now the sky is broken, door by door.
Strangers in the room obscure the hosts.
The meadow is not guarded any more
By watchers coming lonely to their posts.

The animals are never to be named
That swarm beyond our company of old:
Stragglers from the herd, that we had tamed
Unknowing the recesses of the fold.

Those were no heroes whom we once addressed:
Hercules, Orion, and the Twins.
Unwounded, they were running from the rest
Far there where only now the war begins.

There is a game for players still to play,
Pretending that the board was never lost.
But still the painted counters will decay,
And knowledge sit along to count the cost.

The God of Galaxies

The god of galaxies has more to govern
Than the first men imagined, when one mountain
Trumpeted his anger, and one rainbow,
Red in the east, restored them to his love.
One earth it was, with big and lesser torches,
And stars by night for candles. And he spoke
To single persons, sitting in their tents.

Now streams of worlds, now powdery great whirlwinds
Of universes far enough away
To seem but fog-wisps in a bank of night
So measureless the mind can sicken, trying—
Now seas of darkness, shoreless, on and on
Encircled by themselves, yet washing farther
Than the last triple sun, revolving, shows.

The god of galaxies—how shall we praise him?
For so we must, or wither. Yet what word
Of words? And where to send it, on which night
Of winter stars, of summer, or by autumn
In the first evening of the Pleiades?
The god of galaxies, of burning gases,
May have forgotten Leo and the Bull.

But God remembers, and is everywhere.
He even is the void, where nothing shines.
He is the absence of his own reflection
In the deep gulf; he is the dusky cinder
Of pure fire in its prime; he is the place
Prepared for hugest planets: black idea,
Brooding between fierce poles he keeps apart.

Those altitudes and oceans, though, with islands
Drifting, blown immense as by a wind,
And yet no wind; and not one blazing coast
Where thought could live, could listen—oh, what word
Of words? Let us consider it in terror,
And say it without voice. Praise universes
Numberless. Praise all of them. Praise Him.

Down World

No animal so flattens to the ground,
Hiding and sliding, as clear water will:
Its belly nowhere different from the back
Of the sloped earth it hugs, head downward still.

Spineless, it takes all shapes except the serpent's
With his neck hooped, when anger in him stares.
Water is faceless; for it leaves its features,
Spendthrift, on the very stone it wears.

Men cannot pick it up, the stubborn creeper.
Jointless it lies, head downward, sucking sand.
Yet they will try; there is no older plaything
Than gravity delayed, than banking land,

Than the filled gulch, than levelness extended
Till a wave backward laps, till boats can ride.
So the dam holds. But deep at its foundation
Heave the sunk shoulders, not to be denied.

The sodden eyelids, weary of themselves,
Dream of the crack to come, the pouring through;
Then the parched bed, abrasive, and the close
Going once again down world and true.

Woman Few of Words

Lady, excellently brief
(Let me be too),
The sweet things you say
Are salt also,
For true.

It takes my very breath, the mixing,
As if I tried
To be both hot and cold
Together; lived,
And died.

As if within a summer sky
Some lightning hid;
Not to be found except
As on love's day
You did.

Sonnet XXVIII

Never to be renewed or to increase,
And never to be changed from what it was:
The love that was the maker of this lease
Was love-upon-first-sight, whom all the laws
Of happiness obey, and kingdoms coming
Choose to be the glory of their thrones.
He is the oldest love, he is the humming
Of these incessant bees among my bones;
He is the senses' king; my youngest thought
He molds before I know it has been born;
He is the flesh's despot; the inwrought,
Deep joy; or in my side the sudden thorn.
    Oh, strange that on that day I was so strong,
    Bearing him all at once; and now so long!

My Poor Love

Keep up your humming, west wind, and your silly
Songs, you birds; and all you trees, half bent
With sound, keep whispering to the grass, the ground.

Keep noisy, world; yet leave one little crack
For silence to slip through you, one thin cleft,
One hollow vein that my poor love can follow.

My poor love, it cannot cry—not loud
It cannot, nor so sweet as those small sparrows,
Piping, nor so warm as her eyes, weeping.

There she waits—oh, I know where—and truly
Listens—O my love, she truly leans
And listens; for my silence here she listens.

Let it go then, wind and thunder, let it
Pass between you, songbirds, let it pierce you,
Trees, like words upon the wing—oh, these.

Private Worship

She lay there in the stone folds of his life
Like a blue flower in granite. This he knew;
And knew how now inextricably the petals
Clung to the rock; recessed beyond his hand-thrust;
More deeply in, past more forgotten windings
Than his rude tongue could utter, praising her.

He praised her with his eyes, beholding oddly
Not what another saw, but what she added,
Thinning today and shattering with a slow smile,
To the small flower within, to the saved secret.
She was not his to have; except that something,
Always like petals falling, entered him.

She was not his to keep—except the brightness,
Flowing from her, that lived in him like dew;
And the kind flesh he could remember touching,
And the unconscious lips, and both her eyes:
These lay in him like leaves, beyond the last turn
Breathing the rocky darkness till it bloomed.

It was not large, this chamber of the blue flower,
Nor could the scent escape; nor the least color
Ebb from that place and stain the outer stone.
Nothing upon his grey sides told the fable,
Nothing of love or lightness, nothing of song;
Nothing of her at all. Yet he could fancy—

Oh, he could feel where petals spread their softness,
Gathered from windfalls of her when she smiled;
Growing some days, he thought, as if to burst him—
Oh, he could see the split halves, and the torn flower
Fluttering in sudden sun; and see the great stain—
Oh, he could see what tears had done to stone.

Proper Clay

Their little room grew light with cries;
He woke and heard them thread the dark,
He woke and felt them like the rays
Of some unlawful dawn at work:

Some random sunrise, lost and small,
That found the room's heart, vein by vein.
But she was whispering to the wall,
And he must see what she had seen.

He asked her gently, and she wept.
"Oh, I have dreamed the ancient dream.
My time was on me, and I slept;
And I grew greater than I am;

"And lay like dead; but when I lived,
Three wingèd midwives wrapped the child.
It was a god that I had loved,
It was a hero I had held.

"Stretch out your mortal hands, I beg.
Say common sentences to me.
Lie cold and still, that I may brag
How close I am to proper clay.

"Let this within me hear the truth.
Speak loud to it." He stopped her lips.
He smoothed the covers over both.
It was a dream perhaps, perhaps,

Yet why this radiance round the room,
And why this trembling at her waist?
And then he smiled. It was the same
Undoubted flesh that he had kissed;

She lay unchanged from what she was,
She cried as ever woman cried.
Yet why this light along his brows?
And whence the music no one made?

The Sign in the Sky

Look, he said aloud,
My love across the Hollow in your father's
House—look, look! The sky is all one blackest cloud
Filled suddenly with fire, soft fire.
Look, my love, look now!

This was long ago,
And the man is dead. But on that day of days
She too was at her window, wondering; and so
She saw—and cried to him across the Hollow,
Look, dear love, look now!

Time even then was old,
And she is dead. But there has never been
Another day like that one, when a rain of gold,
Falling without falling, woke two lovers:
Now! Let it be now!

They were but neighbors then,
And both are dead. But at that burning hour,
With all the world around them rosy red, they ran
And ran, and met midway the Hollow meadows:
Now! My darling, now!

The moment never stays.
Nobody now remembers them as one
From that day on to death, that darkest day of days
When suddenly high fire consumed their doubt
And now! each answered, now!

Winter Tryst

When the Atlantic upsloped itself
Like roofs of higher and higher houses,
To the great ridge, the foaming shelf
Whereon no dolphin ever browses;

When the wild grey broke into white,
And ships rose endward, crushing mountains;
When it was thus, and icy light
Poured up from phosphorescent fountains:

When it was thus, at winter's crest,
A vessel arrived; and the annual ocean,
Faithfully setting her down in the west,
Repented awhile of its furious motion;

Subsided; but only until that prow
Was pointed again, and a passenger, waving,
Wept in the channel, reminded now
Of eleven months, and the duty of braving

A spring and a summer, and longer fall
Till the month of the year that was set for returning;
Then the grey slopes; and the port, and the tall
Still lover—O time! O bitter adjourning!

When the Atlantic upheaved its whole
And the bottomless world dared keels to try it:
Then was the season; this poor soul
Only that month kept longing quiet.

Only that month: most difficult,
Most dark. Most loveless, and most unable.
Yet it was hers. And time's result
Is love's most fair, most speechless fable.

Then Both Shall Be

When icicles around the earth
Are played upon by one long wind,
And crickets winter in warm grass,
Then I shall be as once I was.

When midnight mushrooms march away
And owls are motherly to mice,
And there is only one great star,
Then you will be as once you were.

When rocks remember being fire
And time to come ticks on the wall,
And truth is mirror of each man,
Then both shall be as both have been.

And Not My Wounds

Tell him I was beautiful,
Tell him I walked well;
Tell him I was columbine,
Brown daisy, and harebell.

He talked of these things that I was,
And called the world to see,
Like one who had created them,
Then manufactured me.

Tell him I am stars by night,
And stillness by noonday.
For he must know, that left me here,
Nothing has gone away;

Nothing is dead or different—
Tell him, and make sure.
For he must understand that I
And not my wounds endure.

Unresponsive

I love you as a bee loves
Plums. Please look at me, she said.
All these years, and almost never
Have you even turned your head.

My life! But he couldn't say it so she heard.
This busy frown, this stiff
Walking away from the one sound
That moved him most—
I love you more than Jupiter or Mars—
It was perverse,
Or worse.

Her very eyes were stars,
And he did not look up.
Her voice was purest music,
And he stood like stone.
When would it break out of him,
The fire of his delight?
Some time it might.

Be careful, though, after so many years.
She is still with me, warm and bright,
By day, by night.
Better not step too suddenly
Out of twilight.

The Bitterest Things

The bitterest things are sweets misunderstood,
Or worse, refused in fury: the struck face
Of Desdemona, doubted; the searched word
More innocent than milk, but by this madness
Curdled; such a forearm as Diana
Shed once like a shadow over pain
Chopped into lecher's meat, the eye despising
What is most whole, most his, the heart distributing
Minced gifts to others; jealous generosity
Letting the benefactor's own best blood.
The bitterest is the purest; but mistaken,
Most poisonous. To her, and then to him.
For he is last to know what lavish gold
He vinagered, what water, brackish now,
Is spiderless no more; and that he drinks it.

Little Trip

Let's go. Let's be somewhere awhile
We haven't ever been before;
And strangers cut the random grass
Or leave it ragged. That can pass;
For now the road climbs more and more,
And we are silent mile by mile
Between whose woods? We'll never know
Unless we stop to read his name.
Up and over, down and on
Around this mountain, blue then brown.
Here is a river, wild or tame
According as the rocks below
Be few or many. Next a house,
And neat or not we like it well,
For someone else does all the chores
Or doesn't do them. Churches, stores—
There, I heard the crossing bell.
So home by dark to moth and mouse.

To a Child with Eyes

Footprints now on bread or cake
Merely are what a mouse can make.
You cannot open any door
And find a brownie on the floor,
Or on the window where he went,
A fork, a spoon, a finger-dent.
Farmers climbing from the mow
Surprise no imp beneath a cow,
Milking madly. Breakfast bells
Are never tinkled from dry wells.
The commonwealth is gone that shut
Its felons in a hazelnut.
Forests are no longer full
Of fairy women who can pull
A leaf around them, and can dance
Upon the very breath of plants.
River rocks are bare of men
Who wring their beards and dive again.
Is there nothing left to see?
There is the squirrel. There is the bee.
There is the chipmunk on the wall,
And the first yellow every fall.
There is the hummingbird, the crow.
There is the lantern on the snow.
There is the new-appearing corn.
There is the colt a minute born.
Run and see, and say how many.
There are more if there is any.

The Child at Winter Sunset

The child at winter sunset,
Holding her breath in adoration of the peacock's tail
That spread its red—ah, higher and higher—
Wept suddenly. "It's going!"

The great fan folded;
Shortened; and at last no longer fought the cold, the dark.
And she on the lawn, comfortless by her father,
Shivered, shivered. "It's gone!"

"Yes, this time. But wait,
Darling. There will be other nights—some of them even
      better."
"Oh, no. It died." He laughed. But she did not.
It was her first glory.

Laid away now in its terrible
Lead coffin, it was the first brightness she had ever
Mourned. "Oh, no, it's dead." And he her father
Mourned too, for more to come.

He's Coming

He's coming. He just called. Said he was coming,
Maybe, right away. O southern river,
Kiss that trestle sweetly,
Rub that upright gently,
And keep no train from home.

He's coming. Said all papers would be signed
By Sunday. O you honeysuckle timber.
Wrap those tulips, redbuds,
Hold those oaks from falling
Down on the right of way.

He's coming. Said expect him. There! what music
Rails already make, and pounded switches:
Wheels inside the south wind.
Where? O you the south wind,
Keep soft and strong today.

Young Woman at a Window

Who so valiant to decide?
Who so prompt and proper-active?
Yet each muscle in her brain
Relaxes now; is unrestrictive;
Lets her lean upon this dark
November night wind; lets it work—

Oh, lets it ask her if she thinks,
Oh, lets it whisper if she knows
How much of time is like a stream
Down which her headless body flows;
How many answers, proudly made,
Will be like minnows overlaid

With inch on inch of glossy black,
With depth on depth of sliding water;
Lets it dare her to predict
Those floods of silence coming later;
Till she melts, and leaning long
Is only conscious of wind-song.

Who so valorous of voice?
Who so staunch upon the ground?
But wind-and-water-song at work
Stops both her ears against the sound
Of someone here she used to know;
Of someone saying: It is so.

She leans and loses every word.
Her loudest wisdom well is gone.
But still the current of the night
Comes with its foaming on and on;
Pours round the sill; dissolves the hands;
And still the dreamless body stands.

The Ancient Couple on Lu Mountain

Into the pool of silence our tears made,
Our secret tears when lord son went away—
How straight his back among the willows was!—
Into this lake of time whereon our house
Is a small hidden island, nevertheless
Sound falls: a single dropping of sweet words,
With every moon, into this upland sea
That no crane visits, for the shores are lost.

Lord son is faithful. With each full of the moon
A letter comes here from the capital:
Comes dripping, dripping its clear characters
Like raindrops, one by one, into soft water.
No silence then. Yet afterward! yet now,
When the moon wanes; when memory grows weaker
Of the few musical, pure drops. How deep this pool is
Only the dark cranes know that never come.

Parents' Recompense

Those that we hovered,
Holding our breath,
Suddenly see him,
Granduncle Death,
Walking close by.
So we are to die.

Not yet. We are strong.
But it is their turn
To indicate love
By excess of concern.
They do; and we smile
All the last mile.

Sleep, Grandmother

Sleep, grandmother, sleep.
The rocking chair is ready to go,
And harness bells are hung in a row
As once you heard them
In soft snow.

Sleep, grandmother, sleep.
Your sons are little and silly again;
Your daughters are five and seven and ten;
And he that is gone
Was not gone then.

Sleep, grandmother, sleep.
The sleigh comes out of the winter woods
And carries you all in boots and hoods
To town for candy
And white dress goods.

Sleep, grandmother, sleep.
The rocking chair is old as the floor,
But there he nods, at the noisy door,
For you to be dancing
One dance more.

The First Snow of the Year

The old man, listening to the careful
Steps of his old wife as up she came,
Up, up, so slowly, then her slippered
Progress down the long hall to their door—

Outside the wind, wilder suddenly,
Whirled the first snow of the year; danced
Round and round with it, coming closer
And closer, peppering the panes; now here she was—

Said "Ah, my dear, remember?" But his tray
Took all of her attention, having to hold it
Level. "Ah, my dear, don't you remember?"
"What?" "That time we walked in the white woods."

She handed him his napkin; felt the glass
To make sure the milk in it was warm;
Sat down; got up again; brought comb and brush
To tidy his top hair. "Yes, I remember."

He wondered if she saw now what he did.
Possibly not. An afternoon so windless,
The huge flakes rustled upon each other,
Filling the woods, the world, with cold, cold—

They shivered, having a long way to go,
And then their mittens touched; and touched again;
Their eyes, trying not to meet, did meet;
They stopped, and in the cold held out their arms

Till she came into his: awkwardly,
As girl to boy that never kissed before.
The woods, the darkening world, so cold, so cold,
While these two burned together. He remembered,

And wondered if she did, how like a sting,
A hidden heat it was; while there they stood
And trembled, and the snow made statues of them.
"Ah, my dear, remember?" "Yes, I do."

She rocked and thought: he wants me to say something.
But we said nothing then. The main thing is,
I'm with him still; he calls me and I come.
But slowly. Time makes sluggards of us all.

"Yes, I do remember." The wild wind
Was louder, but a sweetness in her speaking
Stung him, and he heard. While round and round
The first snow of the year danced on the lawn.

Bailey's Hands

The right one that he gave me—
I could have shut my eyes
And heard all seventy summers
Rasping at their scythes.

The left one that he lifted,
Tightening his hat—
I could have seen the cut groves
Lie fallen, green and flat;

Or seen a row of handles,
Ash-white and knuckle-worn,
Run back as far as boyhood
And the first field of thorn:

The two-edged axe and sickle,
The pick, the bar, the spade,
The adze, and the long shovel—
Their heads in order laid,

Extending many an autumn
And whitening into bone,
As if the past were marching,
Stone after stone.

So by his hands' old hardness,
And the slow way they waved,
I understood the story:
Snath-written, helve-engraved.

Bailey's Widow

Still there, as if the weathered house
Were tomb and low memorial; no shaft,
No sky thing, but a hugger of such earth
As he with horizontal craft
Knew webwise; we remember how he kneeled
And studied every silver herb afield.

Still kitchen table bound, by windows
Wiped to keep the headstones far and clear;
Still huge among her trinkets: catalogues,
Gilt cards, rag balls, and cooking gear,
She sits, the clock a goddess overhead
Less watched than watching, like the distant dead:

An old man under gravel, sidewise
Peering; and she rubs the pane to see.
Yet more that he may feel how still the cats
Prowl round her, blinking up; how three
Small dogs dispute the blessing of her lap;
And how she sometimes nods to him by nap.

The Secret Mother

I was there early, I said I would be,
The day the foundlings had to be moved.
One to a woman, they had to be bundled
And carried down Avenue A to a building
So fine and so high—oh, it took your breath
To think of the life, to think of the death.

Nurses and nuns, in white, in black,
Then volunteers: I was one of those.
I said I would be there early, and was.
I thought they would give me a chance to choose,
Seeing I had no child of my own—
But I lied. I had her entirely alone.

Nobody knew she was made, not even
The seaman her father; we met in a street.
It was part of my plan that such be so;
I used him that night, then let him be gone.
He was handsome and good—oh, I thought I was wise;
But who will be with him when he dies?

I thought I was brave; yet I dressed her warm
And left her in Gramercy Park to be found.
I cried, but I left her. Then she was here;
I knew, for I watched. The nurses and nuns
Could never have guessed, that day of the moving,
Who wanted her most—oh, months of loving!

It was foolish to think they would hand her to me.
I reached, but a tall old sister took her;
Walked in the wind that rose, and rocked her
Stiffly; I knew by the habit that swayed.
The baby I carried I never unwrapped;
Never peeked in; it was good, and slept.

There were people that stood, and some of them smiled
At the great one that walked; but none at my daughter,
Deep in her arms—oh, hidden, my heart.

She had laughed when I laughed, she was mirror to me.
She was what I planned when I thought I was brave
And let him be gone. Oh, wind, oh, wave.

Recognition Scene

From many a mile the son,
From a third of the earth the father;
Each of them bearing his sign
Of kinship high as a feather.
Dusky the hour, and late;
What shall we do that wait?

We shall not quit the grove,
We shall not rise and scatter.
Something deep as the grave
Holds every heart in a flutter.
Dewy the night. No bird—
There! Who trembled? Who heard?

Who spied him, tall in the west?
Old is the night, and bitter.
Far in the eastern waste
Who caught a faint hoof and a clatter?
Now closer—now here—he draws—
Oh, insupportable pause!

Return to Ritual

The mother of life indulges all our wandering
Down the lone paths that narrow into peace.
She knows too well the gradual discovery
And the slow turning round until we cease:
Resolved upon the wide road once again
Whose dust hangs over day and mantles men.

Here is the drumming phalanx, here is the multitude;
Listen, and let us watch them over the stile.
We that remember clean moss ways and the tamaracks,
Let us be timorous now and shudder awhile.
We shall be early enough, no matter when,
Mother of dust, O mother of dust and men.

How time passes, here by the wall of eternity!
Even so soon we summon her; we are prepared.
Already these feet are lifting in a wild sympathy;
Who can remember the cool of a day unshared?
Mother of marches, mother, receive us then.
Listen! The dust is humming a song to the men.

The Double Life

Unnamed and named, two men in me,
Mankind and Jack, the root, the rose,
Something unseen, something awhile
Here, thorned and pungent, rash to the wind,
Then there, then where: two men in one,
Nicknamed and nameless, twine together.
Each for himself, yet one is two
When scent is servant to understanding.
Each for the other; and so the old one
Honors the young one, brief, unique.
How would the world know either was here
Except for an image doomed to go?
How could it say whence came this red
Except for the dark unheard idea?
Body and soul, particular both,
Depend in terror each on each;
So wave as one in double pride:
Myself, and he that never died.

Born Brothers

Equality is absolute or no.
Nothing between can stand. We are the sons
Of the same sire, or madness breaks and runs
Through the rude world. Ridiculous our woe
If single pity does not love it. So
Our separate fathers love us. No man shuns
His poorest child's embrace. We are the sons
Of such, or ground and sky are soon to go.

Nor do born brothers judge, as good or ill,
Their being. Each consents and is the same,
Or suddenly sweet winds turn into flame
And floods are on us—fire, earth, water, air
All hideously parted, as his will
Withdraws, no longer fatherly and there.

The Deepest Dream

The deepest dream is of mad governors.
Down, down we feel it, till the very crust
Of the world cracks, and where there was no dust,
Atoms of ruin rise. Confusion stirs,
And fear; and all our thoughts—dark scavengers—
Feed on the center's refuse. Hope is thrust
Like wind away, and love sinks into lust
For merest safety, meanest of levelers.

And then we wake. Or do we? Sleep endures
More than the morning can, when shadows lie
Sharper than mountains, and the cleft is real
Between us and our kings. What sun assures
Our courage, and what evening by and by
Descends to rest us, and perhaps to heal?

Prophet

He did not say anything utterly strange,
At any rate to a thoughtful person.
Why then do we honor him, and call him prophet?

Because he said what we had always understood
When we were alone, when we were thoughtful.
We honor him because he made us remember,

Why, that we ourselves were serious once,
That we were children, and loved peace.
He gave us again the quietness of our minds.

The only strange thing was, his wild look.
But of course it was terrible to be where he had been:
To have dug those utterly simple sentences out of the
    soul's grave.

I Went Among the Mean Streets

I went among the mean streets
Of such a city
As should have moved my wrath;
But it was pity.

I did not count the sad eyes,
They were so many.
I listened for the singing;
There was not any.

O thieves of joy, O thoughtless
Who blink at this,
Beware. There will be judgment,
With witnesses.

The Last Look

The great eyes died around this room;
Died everywhere; no matter what wall's blankness,
He printed a pair of circles on it; filled
All four of them; surviving with a rankness

Terrible now to us, the livers-on;
The more so that we loved him for his quiet.
He was a man most delicate: not loud
Like this, like these round eyes; like this gaunt riot

Of spent, unsmiling gazes; for at the last,
Trying to smile farewell to us, he could not.
So it appeared that day, I mean. We now
Think otherwise. He looked at us and would not.

Why? But if we knew this, we had known
The other man, the man before the illness.
Now that he is a stranger—studying back,
We were unjust, loving him for his stillness.

That was the least of him. The great eyes prove it,
Lingering on these walls, and hanging fire
With the same truth we buried in the box—
Subdued then to the sermon and the choir,

Yet louder; for the concert here of walls
Is music's self, the sound of someone staring
Utterly, at all things, till they spoke.
This man alone was capable of sharing

Ultimate name and number. This is where—
Yes, this is where he lay, and where the ceiling
Said his last word for him; and where his eyes
Still wander past us, listening and feeling.

Death Indeed

So close death flew that when I walked away,
Still trembling, still stopped about the heart,
I walked as two men, and the livelier
Was he that had been stopped for good—yet came on
Standing, and revisits now all places
With someone lesser, with myself, the seen one.
Nobody notices. Which makes me wonder,
Had the wingbeat been final, whether death,
And death indeed, is not the walking on,
Just this way, of the selfsame legs and shoulders
And the fool's face of yesterday; yet lighted,
And with each weakness gone. For him I see
Is perfect in decision; him I hide
Is errorless, is angel. And I ponder,
After so many deaths, how full the world
Must be of his companions; for till then,
That day, I heard no rustle; and now, even,
Nothing I do reveals him. It is death
Indeed that will unfasten him, my friend
Whom no one else can see; and someday no one.

Dr. Johnson

Monster of learning, master judge
Of poems and philosophies,
Of good and bad, of great and small
Men who prowled Fleet Street with him,
And Cheapside, and the Strand—
Within that huge, that blinking
Frightener of babies,
Nevertheless mice played: delights
In miniature—shy loves, true servants,
Friends, and taste of tea—
And nibbling fears, as now,
As now, of horrible death, oh, on hot feet
Presentiments of blank, of worms, of fire;
Of dissolution, Bozzy,
Dissolution.

Variations upon Disaster

The stone lifted,
A little flaming salamander, startled by broad light,
Darts away among wet leaves.

The hay cut,
A spider web that danced between two blowing stalks
Has to be built again.

The tree felled,
Four blue eggs roll out of a robin's nest.
No young this year.

The basket overturned,
A mouse's brood—run, run—so many mouthfuls
For the scampering cats.

The earth quakes,
And villages fall; but rise again when all the dead
Have namesakes: the new children.

History, a hundred feet
Above high tide, comes in unnoticed; customs drown
So painlessly, nobody weeps.

The Dead Sentry

The dead sentry, doubled with an anguish
Now gone in the direction of his gaze,
Still searching, searching for the end of it—
Couldn't I tell him it is over? wondered
The man who had shot him, coming to make sure;
Wondering too—a habit of late—who was he
Before the wild change of war? What house and where,
And who, in which room, would weep the longest, crying
His name in the night? A habit of late; a bad one;
It might be he could never do this again—
Fingering his gun—and the worst part
Was wondering if the dead knew they were dead;
If this one did. "It's over, over!" he shouted.
But still those eyes went feeling for the end.

Time Was When Death

Time was when death
Seemed mountain, or myth;
Alien to world;
Green oceans away.

Time was when the end
Seemed a pouring of sand;
And the last fine grain—
That glittered the most.

Time was; time is;
And this morning death says:
Stand there; I am here;
I am all that will be.

His language is plain:
Very like to my own.
But the one dark word
Is the sound of my name.

Time still is to be
When I am not I.
The speech death makes
Is not special for me.

Poorhouse Dream

Death is a tall horse
With large white feet,
Coming on a slow walk
Down the long street,

Nudging with a soft nose,
Opening the gate.
Up you must climb then,
Lest you be late.

Starting on a slow walk
And never looking round,
He moves; and the great feet
Never make a sound.

Soon it is a road
With the houses far between,
And when a farm is there at last
Children come and lean,

Shouting over fences;
But not as if they knew.
And not a word arrives
Of what they say to you.

On beneath a bright hill
Is water in a trough.
But he is never thirsty,
And you are looking off,

Thinking of the afternoon,
Thinking of the night.
But all the sky is green there,
And all the hours are white.

He will never halt again,
And you will not descend.
You will be content there
Without any end.

The Plague

"Little boy, what ails me, that you walk
So fearfully and far around?
You stare at this white hair
As at a ghost come out of ground.
I am not dead," the old man said;
And smiled, and frowned.

"Oh no, but it is catching, what you have."
He watched him from the windward side.
"I run like anyone;
I keep the distance good and wide."
So you ought, the old man thought,
And inly sighed.

Outly, though, he laughed and looked away.
"Little doctor, this disease—
You know it is but snow
And frosty blood and wits afreeze.
Yet not for you"—he searched him through—
"Save by degrees."

Oldest Cemetery

I go downhill some days to a little room
Where the first people put their souls to sleep,
And where four walls of fallen fieldstone keep
Close rumor of their names, with verses cut
(I lie and read) against forgetful doom.
Remembered, they would rise in fields of rest
As far away as east is from the west;
Or farther, past all compass; for they shut
This wilderness of time, of nature out;
They thought to wake in such a world of light
As no man works for, warned of coming night;
Pure joy and peace it was. And so they put
Each weary soul to bed, with owls and crows
To watch, and weeds to deepen its repose.

Some days I think the end has come and gone.
Sound fell, and they got up, and where they lay
Was nothing now but litter as away
On wings they went and had their dream at last:
The universe was over. Time goes on
As always, and the same birds in the sky
Declare it, but without hope's reason why:
Tick, tick, until the finish. Or, no blast
Of horns was heard, no host of angels passed;
It all was childish error, and these stones
But tilt above time's waste. And whose the bones?
The verses tell. I ponder them, steadfast,
Expectant. No, the end is coming still
For such as these, on this forgotten hill.

The Seven Sleepers

The liberal arts lie eastward of this shore.
Choppy the waves at first. Then the long swells
And the being lost. Oh, centuries of salt
Till the surf booms again, and comes more land.

Not even there, except that old men point
At passes up the mountains. Over which,
Oh, centuries of soil, with olive trees
For twisted shade, and helicons for sound.

Then eastward seas, boned with peninsulas.
Then, orient, the islands; and at last,
The cave, the seven sleepers. Who will rise
And sing to you in numbers till you know

White magic. Which remember. Do you hear?
Oh, universe of sand that you must cross,
And animal the night. But do not rest.
The centuries are stars, and stud the way.

To Homer

Master of ocean stream, those men you made
Were weaker than its waves, its bitter waves
With their deep smell of caverns never sounded.
Out of dry land you made them, out of dust,
Of bronze; and likened them to bees and lions,
And the lean cranes that flew. Smaller than gods,
Feebler than sun and thunder, less than hills
You reared them, and you set them far away,
Little in strength, from their dear native land.
Yet who so strong? For miracle is in them
Still; still their throats produce a music
Angry and long ago; their armor walks
As waves do, never resting; and their wills
Keep liberty no fate would comprehend.
Submissive to decree, they still are crowned,
Princes of themselves, and rule all verse
As one ruled then from Ida. What so strange,
Master of man's littleness, as this,
That still you most augment him? Still you give
Those governed ones the glory. Sovereign men
Through centuries since have been their subjects still;
And wondered at you too, lord of the sea waves.

Hector Dead

Andromache, when Hector fell,
Cried out upon her fate, not his.
He lost but this one thing, the world;
She gained its million miseries.

Without him it was no more round
And perfect, as pure death can be.
A field of wry-shaped fragments wailed,
Each one of them sharp-voiced as she.

A wilderness of woes it was
By which she measured, that long day,
The quietness in his great throat
That once held every dog away.

To Chaucer

Those waves of understanding that arrived
Were the least ones. You let the long swells go
In their own darkness on around the world
Till they piled high and broke in afterwoe.

For you the choppy ones the sun had wrinkled.
They had come far too, and they still come on.
But in you then they rested. You gave forth
The sound they seek, of old men young at dawn;

Of men that have forgotten nothing woeful,
Yet at their waking smile. The world is fool
Forever, and its tears are not to cease.
But neither is this birdsong, high and cool,

This answer, like your own, to those least waves
That come with sunwarmth dappled on their crests:
The ones unseen except by old late men
And silly larks, up early in their nests.

To the Author of Hesperides *and* Noble Numbers

Herrick, hello.
You cannot be asleep; and yet if so,
Kinsman, your book is not: the lyric
Spring, unquenchable, of him I know,
Robert, as my Herrick.

And I am his,
And therefore yours, like those nine mistresses
Who never spoke one word, yet wore
The crimson ribands and the stomachers
You still I think adore.

I do but read,
Herrick, I do but listen; yet indeed
All that you asked was eyes and ears.
Well, mine are thine, and I shall intercede
With others to give theirs.

Herrick, be sure
Your maids, your meadows, and your verse endure,
And your delicious lewdness, drawn
By the same sun, that loves impure with pure,
From him I dote upon.

Thomas Hardy, Poet

With older eyes than any Roman had
In a stone hole, or Briton under barrow,
Steadily he gazed; and bleakest worlds
Grew warm—illicitly grew warm and moved;
For hope in him was backward, and love narrow.

Belief in him but squinted; God had died
Of palsy, and mankind, alone with feeling,
Was a poor skinless thing. Yet maids and squires,
Ghosts, organists, and gypsies, and small clerks
Mused in his tales, and oxen kept on kneeling.

It was a late hour and cold when he looked out:
The last man that remembered country singing.
And first to call it pitiful. Those folk
Outstayed themselves, he said. Yet as he listened,
Wanly, what sweet bell tongues took to swinging!

And So It Was

And so it was
That Achilles, wounded of mind, called to his beautiful
    mother.
His honor had been hurt, and she must heal it.
She did; but opened a deeper wound, the death of Patroclus;
Whence rivers of blood in which all Troy was drowned.

And so it was
That Odysseus, grizzled darling of Pallas Athene,
Triumphed over the waves; then on dry land,
His enemies. But the grey waves, still reaching, rocked him
Nightly, and robbed the old fox of his rest.

And so it was
That Hamlet, friend of angels, was elected by the fiend
To weed the bed of Denmark, and plucked up,
Before he knew it, flowers; till all was waste
And woe, and the prince of roses died himself by prick of
    thorn.

And so it was
That once in poor La Mancha thought grew rich,
Put forth, and filled the world; which, being full
Already, groaned aloud, fearful of surplus; and the vine,
Weary of its own leaves at last, withdrew.

And so it was
And is, and will be ever: no good man but finds the going
Strange; and yet he goes; and we that watch him
Wish we too had gone where wolf and worm,
Surprising a brave soul, work out their wonders.

My Great Friends

My great friends do not know me.
Hamlet in the halls,
Achilles by the river, and Don Quixote
Feasting with the Duke see no one there
Like me, like Mark Van Doren, who grows daily
Older while they look not, change not,
Die not save the deaths their masters made.

Those, yes, over and over.
And Bottom stands tremendous,
And Sancho rubs his head, half comprehending
Knighthood, and Malvolio's cold voice
Invites the madhouse hour. These neither die
Nor rise again. They look not, change not,
Only as folly, wonderful, lasts on.

Still my great friends ignore me,
Momently grown older
And dying in the west. They will be there
Forever, gods of the world, my own immortals
Who will not go along. Nor do I ask them.
Let them forever look not, change not,
Die not save as mortals may behold.

Ballad of Little Leaves

When all the little leaves of April
Shivered in their green,
She walked alone and wept. "Alas,
In May I must be queen.

"The frosty beard of old King Luke
Beside me in his bed,
While sweetest Arthur wanders here—
God, let me be dead!"

As if He heard, she fell and lay
A long hour in the ferns;
And dreamed that Arthur's loving hands,
Fearful and free by turns,

Now cold, now hot, unlaced her gown
To feel if she had life.
Her heart beat; and she said to him,
"Take it. I am your wife."

It was no dream. They caught them there
And hung them high in chains
Between two oaks whose little leaves
Died with them in the rains.

The Cat and the Miser

Nothing could have brought him to the door,
This brown, this dripping night,
But the faint noise that did: a plucking,
Plucking at the tight
Copper crosswires of the screen.

He knew. It was the cat:
Her signal to come in.
Or thought he knew, the miser,
As with a groan, a sly grin,
Shuffling, he slid the bolt.

No eyes would have been so welcome,
Staring up and blinking.
But these, the tall thief's—
Oh, oh! the unthinking
Blow, the heavy feet.

Oh, oh! The boxes gone,
The misery. Then here she was:
Pluck, pluck—the sound,
In and out, of delicate claws.
What fiend had listened?

Out there, what sharpened face,
Vigilant, had learned the trick?
He staggered up and let her through.
Late, late! A sudden kick—
But then, caresses.

Foreclosure

So he sat down and slowly, slowly
Worked at his Christian name;
Watching the gold and halfway smiling
As the last letter came;
Till the whole sound was there, and shouted,
Suddenly, his shame.

Between this word then and the other—
His and his father's too—
He stared at the pen as if its handle
Were a great horn, and blew;
Then lowered the point and quietly labored
Till the last ink was through.

So he got up, and through the wide silence
Wandered; and song began.
Not the old tune, for that was buried
Where the slow writing ran;
But remnants, hung in the wind awhile,
And impotent to scan.

There was the bell that once had brought him,
Frightened, across the field;
There was the mad white shepherd's barking,
And the hurt child, unhealed;
There was a hen whose brood came piping
To the red worm revealed.

There was quick trampling on a stairway,
Until doors sealed the sound.
There were the drums of winter booming
When the lame boy was drowned.
So his lost land went with him, pulling
Its tatters close around.

Camp Night

A little water will put out the fire.
But wait. A little wood will keep it breathing.
It is a heart we started with ten sticks
That now are nothing, like a hundred others
Shrunk to this hectic person whose last life
Would drain the whole cool forest if it could.
Another handful, then, though it is late.
So much in little, such a hungry principle:
We are not lightly to extinguish that.
Quiet a little longer, while it hisses
And settles, keeping secret the sore word
That soon enough its embers will forget.
Our own existence, partly. A wild piece
Of me and you we presently must drown.

Little Places

Such power in little places:
The petal weight a coil of jelly moves,
And snails have conquered beaches.
The worm, with neither horn nor bone,
Plows acres.

Prometheus down a cold crack:
Rainstreams freezing, and the granite
Splits; as smoke of sister water
Pushes the long piston; and a copper
Hair holds worlds.

The Yes all year awaited:
Thinnest word, and yet it peoples spring
With mighty houses, lived in; No,
Enormous night; as when the bud bursts
Or does not.

Such power; with plants depending,
Thunder, and small men, and now the spark
Whereby a town is merry.
The end, that neither feels nor sees,
Thanks nothing.

What Fury

What fury in the white sky
Showing over Shepherd's woods!
Look! Is it a kingbird
Or purple martin pouncing so?
There! He almost had the duck hawk
Down. But then he let him go.

Courage? Would you call it that?
Spirit, in a speck as wild
As windy leaf, as falling flake?
Now the updraft—see him rise
And give it to him hard again—
Always aiming at the eyes.

Wrath? Or is it even felt?
Rage at least would have a reason.
Where in such a little brain—
But it is finished. There he went.
He was only playing blazes
In blue air. A spark, and spent.

With Apples

The last leaves are down, and the iron
Trunks, solitary, say they can stand there
Seven cold months without perceptible
Change. But the green ground changes
Daily, so that Hallaway's old horses,
The brown one, the black one,
Nibble at next to nothing where the hoar frost
Of hours ago gave way before the yellow and still blowing,
Blowing—some of them purple—leaves.
These move, head down, but listen:
Someone may be coming, even now, in the bright wind,
With apples. I am coming.
Four pockets full, and extras on the hip.
Hi, there, Handsome Jerry!
Don't you know me, Slobbery Mack?

Nap

I lay me down, but down is deep
Past dark, past death, past deep's idea;
Is the soft seas themselves, that drain
Away as my own mind does, my own
Bones that will not be, not be
Again; not be my bones; not my
Own bones, that settle separately,
Softly, down and down—oh, sweet
Non-being, not my own, wherein
I sink like light in water, dimming
Slowly, oh, so slowly, deep
By deep, beyond the dark of death's idea.

The Fields of November

The fields of November
Fit like a lion's hide:
Old, dreaming lion,
Cold, sleepy ground.

The hollows and the rises,
The boulders, the long swells,
All of them are one there,
Breathing under brown.

But faint breath, and slow beat:
The fields of November
Fit like a warm skin
The dark of the world.

December Setting

What death more wonderful
Than day's in winter?
All the cold west burns,
Burns to be near its insatiable lover,
The dark.

Cunning with hunger,
The two of them mingle
Their hectics—fiery,
Fiery the fusion, and smoky, of living
And lifeless.

Oh, the white heat of it,
Tempered to crimson:
And crimson—oh, lovers,
Oh, lovers of dying—to terrible black
Under black.

Dialogue in December

In so much dark no light is little.
    But can light be at the end of the year?
Only listen. It will come.
    And put out dying? And put out fear?
Yes, but listen. Good heart, listen.
    I do, I do—I see, I hear.

That star is enough in this much night.
    It glitters. But a child has cried.
He is the first one in the world.
    Even the old world, that died?
Even the new—he is all the living.
    And all the dead—are they satisfied?

Listen and look. Is there any weeping?
    Only for comfort, only for joy.
Only for love. But the child that was crying—
    He is a beautiful, strange boy.
He is little and weak, this lord of the world.
    But oh, too strong, too strong to destroy.

Wish for the World

Wish for the world that it will never change,
Even if terrible, to total strange.
Even if good, may there be no excess
Beyond this power to think of more, of less,
That is our lone reward for living here.
May only what is missing still be clear
On any earth to come, that so can teach
Hell's difference, and heaven's—each from each,
And both from its dear self: the single place
Than which all others have exacter grace,
And yet it is the measure. Be it thus
Forever, little world that lengthens us.

Praise Doubt

Praise the good angel doubt,
Guardian of us that walk
On the deep waters of this world.

Praise him. He never rests,
However weary the way
Over these dark, salt, dangerous meadows.

Do not look down, he says;
Beware with me and the sun
Of faith's innumerable caverns.

Monsters can be there.
You will have plenty of time.
Too soon descending, you are devoured.

Praise him. He believes
In the long day we are given.
Praise him. He dances upon the whitecaps.

When the World Ends

When the world ends it is too much to hope,
And yet I do, that neither knife nor rope,
Nor sudden flame, nor worse than sudden freeze,
Is executioner. No less than these
Implacable, what if gold autumn came
And stayed till it was weary—spread the same
Cool hectic over waters and wild boughs
That now arrives for but a week's carouse;
Then winter? What if such a wonder fall
Kept on as if it were the end, the all?
What if it were, and centuries of red
So flushed each field and roof and river bed
That death itself lay down, and nothing died
Till all things did, beneath a shower as wide
As oceans of together-dropping leaves?
What if it were, and still no late reprieves
Canceled the utter end? I do not keep
That hope; and yet I dream of this slow sleep,
This indolent, this all but evermore
October such as never came before.

Comedy

The world will not be understood.
Put on a sword, put on a hood.
Listen. Can you hear me? Good.
The world will not be understood.

Tragedy

The world is something I must try,
However hard, however high.
Though I stumble, though I die,
The world is something I must try.

Eternity's Low Voice

Eternity's low voice,
That no one yet has heard,
Sings peace be with you, children
Of man, beast, worm, and bird.

Warning

God will be hard to love.
Nature does not assist.
She was the jealous one
When daylight and chaos kissed.

Born Equal

"Born equal? When so many—
Look round you—are inferior?
In God's name who believes"—
"None but the superior."

Freedom

To be what no one ever was,
To be what everyone has been:
Freedom is the mean of those
Extremes that fence all effort in.

Tourist

I passed Olympus in the night,
But had I passed by day
I still could tell you less of it
Than blind Homer may.

Cold Beauty

Woods, flaming in winter sunset,
Had best be witnessed warm indoors.
There is no heat in all that hectic;
Nor—wait, child—from Orion's stars.

Morning Assignment

A woman, sitting and sewing in south window light,
Is silent, and so is the small granddaughter by her side,
Counting not stitches, no, but yellow and red and white
Buttons, and silver snaps, and ribbons fit for a bride.

Goldfinches

The hayfield is not afire,
Yet sparks fly upward.
Crisscross then, and looping,
They dive down backward.

Indomitable

The chickadee the cat clawed
Is here this morning on one leg.
With no tailfeathers left he lights
And, balancing, begins to beg.

No Communication

The wren that rages when I sit
Too close to this crabapple tree
Cannot be told, for all her wit,
I hung the gourd she guards from me.

End

This bird died flying,
And fell in flowers.
Oh, what a world
Went with him. Ours.

Good Appetite

Of breakfast, then of walking to the pond;
Of wind, work, rain, and sleep I never tire.
God of monotony, may you be fond
Of me and these forever, and wood fire.

Epitaph

Let this be true, that I have loved
All men and things both here and gone;
But most the men whose love surpassed
My love, and so lives on and on.

Index of Titles

Index of First Lines

AMERICAN CENTURY SERIES